eat.shop chicago 3rd edition

an encapsulated view of the most interesting, inspired and authentic
locally owned eating and shopping establishments in chicago, illinois

researched, photographed and written by anna h. blessing

cabazon books : 2009

table of contents

eat

shop

anna's notes on chicago

Something's up in Chicago. There's beer and pizza, sports and politics—but NOT as usual. When I talk politics, I'm talking President of the United States. When it comes to sports, I'm thinking 2016 Olympics. And as for this town's traditional fare? *Hot Doug's* dogs, *Great Lake*'s pizza and *Kuma's Corner*'s burgers are so popular that you are almost guaranteed a queue with a bunch of hungry hounds itching for these re-imagined Windy City classics.

Out-of-towners have been lining up for large-scale eateries and name brand shops in Chicago for years, but it's a new phenomenon that people are seeking out off-the-beaten-path local treasures. Travelers and locals alike are paying serious attention to this city's outstanding local shops and eateries. If Barack Obama, Frank Gehry and Renzo Piano have played a part in creating a Chicago buzz, it's no doubt the fantastic local businesses you'll find in this book that have kept the excitement building.

Chicago has been dubbed the third coast and the second city, but it seems like this town is moving its way to first place. Find yourself at any of the spots on the following pages and you'll be experiencing businesses that stand up to the best in the world, in my humble (and always hungry!) opinion.

Outside of the world of eating and shopping, here are a few of my favorite things in Chicago:

1 > *The River*: Amazing bridges, a fascinating history, fantastic city views and an expanded riverwalk with outdoor cafes. And you thought the lake was great.

2 > *The Alfred Caldwell Lily Pool:* It's hard to narrow down what I like best about expansive Lincoln Park, but this hidden haven has to be it.

3 > *Architecture*: I'm sweet on SOM's Hancock, Goldberg's Marina City and Mies' LSD buildings, but this is just a snippet—the architectural wonders of Chicago are endless.

4 > *Millennium Park:* I never tire of it—tennis on the courts, a swing around the shiny bean, a walk through Lurie Garden, or a meander over the snaking walkway. And now there's a new bridge to the gorgeous new Modern Wing of the Art Institute.

5 > *The Mayor*: His love for the city and his drive to make it a world leader are endless. He's our hero, knight and city savior!

about eat.shop

• All of the businesses featured in this book are locally owned and operated. In deciding which businesses to feature, we require this criteria first and foremost. Then we look for businesses that strike us as utterly authentic, and uniquely conceived, whether they be new or old, chic or funky. We are not an advertorial guide, therefore businesses do not pay to be featured.

• The maps in this guide are not highly detailed but instead are representational of each area noted. We suggest, if you are visiting, to also have a more detailed map. Streetwise Maps are always a good bet, and are easy to fold up and take along with you. Explore from neighborhood to neighborhood. Note that almost every neighborhood featured has dozens of great stores and restaurants other than our favorites listed in this book. We also have a Google map of Chicago with the indicators of the businesses noted at: http://tiny.cc/kUO94. Paste this into the browser of your smart phone, it's quite useful.

• Make sure to double check the hours of the business before you go by calling or visiting its website. Often the businesses change their hours seasonally. The pictures and descriptions of each business are representational—please don't be distraught when the business no longer carries or is not serving something you saw or read about in the guide.

• Small local businesses have always had to work that much harder to keep their heads above water. During these rough economic times, many will close. We apologize if some of the businesses featured here are no longer open. The more you visit the businesses in this book, the better chance they have at staying open.

• The *eat.shop* clan consists of a small crew of creative types who travel extensively and have dedicated themselves to great eating and interesting shopping around the world. Each of these people writes, photographs and researches his or her own books.

• Please support the indie bookstores in Chicago. To find these bookstores, use this great source: www.indiebound.org/indie-store-finder.

• *eat.shop* supports the *3/50 project* (www.the350project.net) and in honor of it have begun our own challenge (please see the back inside cover of this book).

• There are three ranges of prices noted for restaurants, $ = cheap, $$ = medium, $$$ = expensive

previous edition businesses

eat

angel food bakery
athenian room
avec
bistro campagne
blackbird
bongo room
bonsoiree
bourgeois pig
bricks
chalkboard
coco rouge
cru cfae and wine bar
custom house
de cero
fat willy's rib shack
flo
follia
fonda del mar
fox & obel
frontera grill
green zebra
hai yen
hotchocolate
intelligentsia
irazu
jane's
japonais
jin ju
la creperie
le bouchon

lula café
matchbox
milk & honey café
mirai sushi
mk
moody's pub
naha
pastacceria natalina
pastoral
ping pong
ras dashen
red hen bread
rockit bar & grill
sultan's market
sushi wabi
sweet many b's
tac quick
the bleeding heart bakery
the brown sack
the goddess and grocer
the map room
the original rainbow cone
the silver palm
tizi melloul
tre kronor
tweet
valhalla
vella café
victory's banner
volo

shop

a new leaf
alcalas
american science
blake
eskell
gem
grow
habit
i.d.
ikram
jake
kara mann
komoda
koros
larkspur
lulu's
modlife
nina
ouest
primitive
red dog house
revival
rotofugi
rr#1 chicago
saint alfred
salvage one
stitch
tangerine
the boring store
the house of glunz

the left bank
the painted lady
the red balloon co.
the t-shirt deli
twosided
up down tobacco
white chicago
wolfbat & b-girls
wright

if a previous edition business does not appear on this list, it is either featured again in this edition, has closed or no longer meets our criteria or standards.

a master pdf of the spreads from the previous edition of *eat.shop chicago* is available for download and purchase at www.eatshopguides.com

where to lay your weary head

there are many great places to stay in chicago, but here are a few of my picks:

dana hotel and spa
660 north state street
888.301.3262 / danahotelandspa.com
standard double from $199
restaurants: ajasteak
bars: alibi, vertigo sky lounge
notes: a mod, yet tranquil hotel

hotel felix
111 west huron street
312.447.3440 / hotelfelixchicago.com
standard double from $150
restaurant: elate
notes: brand new green hotel—the city's first leed-certified

w chicago > city center
172 west adams street
312.332.1200 / starwoodhotels.com
standard double from $260
restaurant: ristorante we
bar: the living room bar
notes: reliably stylish hotel—a short walk from the art institute and millennium park

the james hotel
55 east ontario street
877.526.3755 / jameshotels.com
standard double from $239
restaurant: david burke's primehouse
bar: jbar
notes: a focus on good design and art with kiehls products in the rooms

other lodging options > sofitel chicago water tower (sofitel.com), **hotel indigo** (goldcoastchicagohotel.com),
affinia (affinia.com)

notes

90 miles cuban café

cuban joint

3101 north clybourn avenue. between oakley and western. brown line: addison
773.248.2822 www.90milescubancafe.com
mon - sat 8a - 8p sun 9a - 6p

opened in 2008. owners: christine and alberto gonzalez
$-$$: all major credit cards accepted
breakfast. lunch. dinner. first come, first served

roscoe village >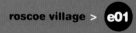

You go 90 miles out from Chicago, you end up, well, somewhere in the middle of Indiana... maybe. You go 90 miles from Miami and you end up Cuba. But, if you go just a few miles north on Clybourn, you end up at *90 Miles Cuban Café*. Here, you can find cubano sandwiches, hot plaintains, café con leche, and a feeling like you've traveled south and found yourself on the island. Christine and Alberto import the flavors of Cuba to us Chicagoans, which makes me very happy, and very full.

imbibe / devour:
malta
iron beer
cubano sandwich
ropa vieja sandwich
maduros
tostones
yuca rellena
papa rellena

big jones

coastal southern cuisine

5347 north clark street. between balmoral and summerdale. red line: berwyn
773.275.5725 www.bigjoneschicago.com
mon - fri 11a - 10p sat 9a - 10p sun 9a - 9p

opened in 2008. owner: chef / owner: paul fehribach
$$-$$$: all major credit cards accepted
lunch. dinner. brunch. reservations recommended

andersonville >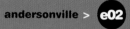

I'm happy that all of the fad food diets—Atkins, South Beach, etc.—are going the way of the dodo, and what people are focusing on more is farm fresh, local, organic ingredients. Frankly, too much worrying about what is and isn't too fattening or carb-rich makes eating lackluster and people grumpy because there isn't much room for eating things like, say, Mississippi mud pie. Or fried anything. What *Big Jones* advocates is a new style of Southern comfort food, which is beautifully prepared and sourced, but doesn't have the life sucked out of it on a quest for no fat. I'm going on the *Big Jones* diet.

imbibe / devour:
peter's sazerac
mint julep
lump blue crab cakes
fried green tomatoes
gumbo du jour
carolina pulled pork
fried catfish
mississippi mud pie

birrieria reyes de ocotlán

la major birria de todo el mundo
1322 west 18th street. between between ada and blue island. pink line: 18th
312.733.2613
mon - fri 9a - 8p sat - sun 7a - 8p

opened in 1978. owners: the reyes family
$: cash only
lunch. dinner. first come, first served

You might find yourself on 18th street in Pilsen, knowing that somewhere in this neighborhood there is a darn good taco just waiting for you. There are, in fact, many delicious tacos in this hood, and a constant debate as to which taco is tops. There isn't much of a debate, however, as to which place earns the title Best Goat Taco—that honor goes to *Birreria Reyes de Ocotlán*. From the moment you see the goat painted on the window, you know what to order. Pair the goat taco with some goat stew and you've got yourself one hearty lunch.

mbibe / devour:
horchata
piña jamaica
birria de res (beef) taco
birria de chivo (goat) taco
lengua (tongue) taco
goat stew
mexican rice
tortillas

chickpea

palestinian cafe

2018 west chicago avenue. between damen and hoyne. blue line: division
773-384-9930 www.chickpeaonthego.com
daily 11a - 10p

opened in 2008. owner: amni suqi
$-$$: cash only
lunch. dinner. first come, first served

west town > **e04**

Ah, the glorious chickpea. Mashed, pureed, sautéed, crisped, baked or fried, I will take it any way it is served, but most of all, I will take it at its' namesake restaurant, *Chickpea*. This family business is run by Palestinian natives, with mom in the kitchen making home-cooked food the way her sons love it. Lucky for all of us that the sons are willing to share their mom's cooking talents. Just be sure to clean your plate, or you might get a talking to from the lady in charge. No worries, this is the kind of place you won't want to leave a single morsel behind.

imbibe / devour:
vinto cream soda
arabian tea
hummus
falafel sandwich
fasoolya
mujaddara
malfoof
baklawa

cipollina

italian deli

1543 north damen avenue. between north and schiller. blue line: damen
773.227.6300 www.cipollinadeli.com
mon - fri 8a - 7p sat 8a - 5p sun 8a - 4p

opened in 2008. owner: carol watson
$-$$: all major credit cards accepted
breakfast. lunch. first come, first served

wicker park > **e05**

I grew up in a family that takes their sandwiches very seriously, so when a sandwich shop opens, I'm always just a little bit skeptical. On every occasion I've visited *Cipollina,* it has never failed to deliver an amazing sandwich. Note to you delicate eaters: these beauties are not for those who like a slim stacked sandwich, but rather for those looking for a hefty sandwich packed full of meat and veg and cheese and vinegary pickled items. It's a requirement to have a mouth that's capable of major extension. Good luck, and enjoy!

imbibe / devour:
espresso
housemade italian soda
nutella & banana on toasted ciabatta
four cheese panino
italian sandwich with housemade giardiniera
marinated artichoke sandwich
pastries & cookies
gelato

crisp

modern korean

2940 north broadway street. between wellington and oakdale
brown / purple lines: diversey
773.697.7610 www.crisponline.com
tue - thu 11:30a - 9p fri - sat 11:30a - 10:30p sun 11:30a - 9p

opened in 2008. owners: jon pazona, doug funke and jason lee chef: jason lee
$-$$: all major credit cards accepted
lunch. dinner. take out. first come, first served

lakeview >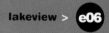

I like a lot of heat in my food. This need for spice runs in the family, as my brother's special drink of choice is vodka on the rocks, loaded with hot peppers, pickles and onions. This is the drink version of getting smacked around. So when I tried the classic crisp bbq fried chicken at the highly addictive modern Korean joint *Crisp*, I asked for a little extra heat. My tastebuds were not disappointed. Since then, I've been eyeing the suicide sauce bird—but I'm thinking I'll have to take it to go, so I can partner it with a flaming vodka or two.

imbibe / devour:
grape juice drink with sac
tahitian treat
crisp bbq korean fried chicken
seoul sassy korean fried chicken
the buddha bowl
seoul sensation korean burrito
chop of the heap
myon's kimchee

crust

organic wood-oven pizza

2056 west division street. corner of hoyne. blue line: damen
773.235.5511 www.crustorganic.com
see website for hours

opened in 2007. owner: michael altenberg chef: jacinto sanchez
$$: all major credit cards accepted
lunch. dinner. first come, first served

wicker park >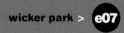

There are warmer, sunnier places to live in the world than Chicago. But if there was sun around all the time, we wouldn't have our annual "coming out" party, which happens during the first week of warm weather and the whole darn city comes out of hiding. It does get a bit dodgy though, as people go cuckoo securing places to eat outdoors. I'll save you the hunt for where to go for al fresco dining: *Crust*. Out on the back patio, guzzling organic beers and wood-oven pizzas, Chicagoans and visitors alike will get what makes a few million people stick around here through the god-forsaken winters.

imbibe / devour:
three floyds gumballhead
two brothers cane & abel
arugula salad
caesar salad
wood-oven pizzas:
  shroom
  wild herb & cheese
  pepperonata

feed

southern soul food

2803 west chicago avenue. corner of california. cta bus: 66-chicago
773.489.4600 www.feedrestaurantchicago.com
mon - fri 8a - 10p sat 9a - 10p sun 9a - 9p

opened in 2006. owners: donna knezek and liz sharp
$-$$: cash only
lunch. dinner. brunch. first come, first served

humbodlt park >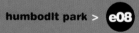

My usually disciplined husband tells me that while living in South Carolina, he would often gorge himself on barbecue and then put himself over the edge eating loads of banana pudding. I couldn't imagine him doing this, until I tasted banana pudding for the first time. *Feed* was my maiden voyage into the realm of this creamy goodness. After a hearty feeding of fried catfish, collard greens and fried green tomatoes, my belly was protruding, yet I was still able to lick up every last taste of the pudding. You don't have to save room for dessert here; but you'll make room for it.

imbibe / devour:
iced tea
1/2 chicken
fried catfish sandwich
really big burger
collard greens
fried okra
corn pudding
banana pudding

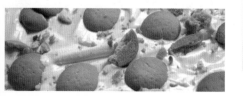

great american cheese collection

a warehouse of great cheese

4727 south talman street. between western and california. orange line: western
773.779.5055 www.greatamericancheese.com
sat 9a - 1p

opened in 1991. owner: giles schnierle
$-$$: all major credit cards accepted
first come, first served

brighton park > **e09**

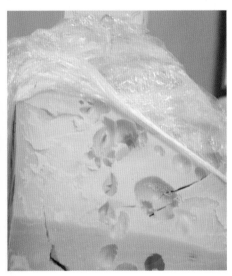

I know what I'll be doing with my saturdays from now on. I'll be heading down to the *Great American Cheese Collection* warehouse. Giles used to sell his cheese solely to a group of the city's best restaurants, but now he's been kind enough to also offer his cheeses to all of us lay folk, working out of a warehouse on the South side, every Saturday. Here are some tips: First, whatever he's offering for sample, you try. Second, you might as well clear your Saturday mornings until the end of time, because one trip in and you'll want to become a regular.

imbibe / devour:
fig salumi
cheese:
   the mayor of nye beach
   sunset bay
   pennsylvania noble mature
   organic caraway gouda
   organic aged cheddar "fait gras"
   aged swiss emmenthaler

great lake

neighborhood pizza joint with a national rep

1477 west balmoral avenue. corner of clark. red line: berwyn
773.334.9270 www.g-lake.com
see website for hours

opened in 2008. owners: lydia esparza and nick lessins
$$: visa. mc
dinner. byo. first come, first served

andersonville > **e10**

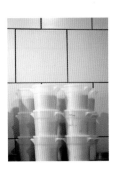

In 1966 journalist Gay Talese wrote a story for Esquire magazine called 'Frank Sinatra Has a Cold.' Assigned to write this profile with a quick deadline, Talese wasn't able to actually interview the singer in time, because Sinatra had a cold. *Great Lake* is my Frank Sinatra. Between the first time I tried their pies and when I tried to shoot them months later, throngs of people had descended on this perfectly appointed Andersonville byo. Getting a good shot of the product became a challenge. I'm thinking you don't need a picture of this perfect pie to convince you to come here though. Just put your trust in me and Frank.

imbibe / devour:
aranciata
pellegrino
pizza:
 tomato, fresh mozzarella, mona, fresh herbs
 cremini mushroom, mona, black pepper
 arugula, pepperoni, mona, fresh cream
mixed greens salad with herb buttermilk

hoosier mama pie company

homemade pie

1618 1/2 west chicago avenue. between ashland and marshfield. blue line: division
312.243.4846 www.hoosiermamapie.com
tue - fri 8a - 7p sat 9a - 5p

opened in 2009. owner: paula haney
$-$$: visa. mc
treats. first come, first served

west town >

Cakes come and go. Cupcakes are so five years ago (though I would never turn one down). But pie... pie is forever. It's classic and dependable, yesterday and tomorrow, oh—and it's very of the moment. How do I know? Well, for one, when Paula opened her little pie shop, it took me days before I could get my hands on a slice—I kept showing up to a sold-out shop. Sad. When I finally did get to dig into a fresh slice, all I could think about was coming back as soon as I could for another sweet, homey, comforting piece of pie. So, *Hoosier Mama*? Pie's your mama.

imbibe / devour:
diner coffee
pies:
   classic apple
   strawberry rhubarb
   banana cream
   lemon meringue
   maple pecan
   chocolate chess

hot doug's

the sausage superstore and encased meat emporium
3324 north california avenue. corner of roscoe. cta bus: 152-addison
773.279.9550 www.hotdougs.com
mon - sat 10:30a - 4p

opened in 2001. chef / owner: doug sohn
$-$$: all major credit cards accepted
lunch. first come, first served

avondale > **e12**

Ever since dressing up as "ketchup" in an elaborate handmade costume for Halloween when I was little (my best friend was "mustard"), I have had a special place in my heart for this condiment. I might have even applied it once to a hot dog, a gaffe and no-no I learned upon moving to Chicago. The thing about *Hot Doug's* is that there is no such thing as a no-no—when there's something like a Mandarin Orange and Teriyaki Chicken Sausage on the menu, you know rules are being broken. Just don't let anyone see you put ketchup on it.

imbibe / devour:
fresca
the elvis
the paul kelly
the keira knightley
the frankie "five angels" pentangelli
the game of the week
duck fat fries (friday & saturday only)
cheese fries

juicy wine company

694 north milwaukee avenue. between carpenter and sangamon. blue line: chicago
312.492.6620 www.juicywine.com
see website for hours

opened in 2006. owner: rodney alex
$$: all major credit cards accepted
wine. light meals. first come, first served

river west > **e13**

The older I get, the harder I find it to relax. There is always something to do, something to check off my numerous lists—I find that I can't just sit back and take it easy. Except when I'm at *Juicy Wine Company*. Rodney seems to be king of taking it easy (damn him), and infuses his whole genius wine/cheese/meats spot with just the right attitude that lets you completely let go and take a load off. At *Juicy Wine*, there is nothing I have to do besides drink more wine, and eat more cheese. These are tasks I'll happily do.

imbibe / devour:
mayberry lemon aide
the velvet devil merlot
saint cosme chateauneuf du pape
betts & scholl barossa valley grenache
the iron fist in a velvet glove pinot noir cheese flight
house-marinated olives
cured meats (especially the finocchiona)
butter & salt

kan pou

thai home cooking and baking

4256 north western avenue. corner of cullom. brown line: western
773.866.2839 www.kanpourestaurant.com
see website for hours

opened in 2008. chef / owner: doungpon morakotjantachote
owner: anuwat morakotjantachote
$-$$: all major credit cards accepted
lunch. dinner. first come, first served

north center > **e14**

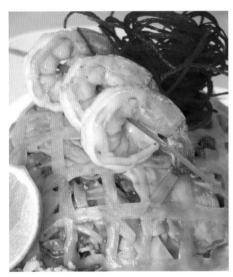

When I first moved here after growing up on the West Coast, I pooh-poohed the Thai food in this city. Ten years later, there are numerous amazing places for Thai cuisine. For example, when *Kan Pou* opened its doors last year, it proved that proximity to Thailand has nothing to do with creating authentic food. Husband and wife duo Doungpon and Anuwat bring the flavors of their homeland to life. And I'll bet you've never tasted a cookie quite as yummy as the Thai spice cookies here. There will be no pooh-poohing *Kan Pou*.

imbibe / devour:
thai ice coffee
mee krob noodle
red wings
panang curry
kan pou ribs
pineapple fried rice
kan pou pad thai
homemade herb cookies

kuma's corner

rock star burgers

2900 west belmont avenue. corner of francisco. blue line: belmont
773.604.8769 www.kumascorner.com
mon - fri 11:30a- 2a sat 11:30a - 3a sun noon - midnight

opened in 2005. owner: owner: michael cain
$$: all major credit cards accepted
lunch. dinner. first come, first served

irving park > **e15**

Here's some advice. If you go to *Kuma's Corner*, whatever hour of the day, any day of the week—don't go with an empty stomach. Most of Chicago is also heading to *Kuma's*, and you'll be waiting in line with a bunch of empty, growling stomachs. Now, here's the tricky part: by the time you get a seat and are ready to order one of these rock star burgers, you will need to famished. These burgers are some serious eating—a strategy is required to get the whole thing down—but there's no doubt, this burger sensation is absolutely worth it and you might not have to eat for a couple of days.

imbibe / devour:
inferno belgian strong ale
surly furious american ipa
burgers:
  "our famous kuma burger"
  black sabbath
  judas priest
p.e.i. mussels
fried calamari

little branch cafe

a sweet little cafe

1251 south prairie avenue. corner of 13th. red line: roosevelt
312.360.0101 www.littlebranchcafe.com
mon - tue 7a - 4p wed - fri 7a - 10p sat 8a - 10p sun 8a - 8p

opened in 2007. owners: soo choi, sang choi and kevin heisner
$$: visa. mc
breakfast. lunch. brunch. first come, first served

Remember the children's book that tells the story of the little baby bird who falls from his nest, loses his mother, then sets out on a quest for home, and memorably asks a steam shovel, "Are you my mother?" I feel a little like this lost bird while searching for a good, homey lunch in Chicago. After several places that didn't fit the bill, I found my home at *Little Branch*. Tucked aways off the beaten path, it might take a bit of looking, but once you find yourself in this sweet little spot, you'll feel as happy as that baby bird who found both his home and his mother.

imbibe / devour:
fruit smoothies
espresso
yogurt parfait
french toast
breakfast frittata sandwich
croissant sandwich
nutella banana sandwich
fig jam prosciutto sandwich

lovely

a bake shop and cafe

1130 north milwaukee avenue. between augusta and division. blue line: division
773.572.4766 www.lovelybakeshop.com
mon - fri 7a - 7p sat 9a - 6p sun 9a - 4p

opened in 2008. owners: brooke dailey and gina heartwig
$-$$: all major credit cards accepted
breakfast. lunch. treats. first come, first served

wicker park > **e17**

On any given day, I swing between realism and pessimism (these days that's not a big swing). Except when I've been to *Lovely*, where my perspective changes to rosy, sweet optimism, and the world seems, well... lovely. I think this is the effect in general of being around baked goods, though this whole place gives off a sort of old timey "gee shucks, ain't life grand," vibe that makes you more than happy to forget your woes. So next time when you're stuck in doom mood, just come to *Lovely* to improve your perspective with a good dose of butter, sugar and eggs.

imbibe / devour:
reed's ginger brew
goose island root beer
pb&j sandwich
blueberry muffin
banana pecan muffin
raspberry linzer coffee cake
chocolate buttercream cake
derby pie

mado

home-cooked mediterranean
1647 north milwaukee avenue. between north and wabansia. blue line: damen
773.342.2340 www.madorestaurantchicago.com
see website for hours

opened in 2008. owners: rob and allie levitt
$$: all major credit cards accepted
dinner. brunch. reservations recommended

wicker park > **e18**

When I'm in high gear researching these books, I tend to get a little tired of eating out. Don't get me wrong, and I certainly don't mean to complain—I get paid to eat good food. But sometimes I just long for a simple, home-cooked meal. Thank goodness for *Mado*. This place feels like I've wandered over to a good friend's house, and it just so happens that the friend is a killer chef, ready to serve up a delicious belly-filling meal. If I can't have home, I'll take *Mado*.

imbibe / devour:
house-cured smelts
sunchokes with lemon & parsley
farm egg bruschetta with bone marrow butter
beef heart with mashed potatoes & red wine
sicilian seafood stew with green olives
spicy pork meatballs with chickpeas & tomato
rainbow trout with arugula, olives & fennel
yogurt sponge pudding

mana food bar

amazing vegetarian food

1742 west division street. between wood and paulina. blue line: division
773.342.1742 www.manafoodbar.com
sun - thu 4 - 10p fri - sat noon - 11p

opened in 2008. owner: susan thompson chef / owner: jill barron
$$: all major credit cards accepted
lunch. dinner. snacks. first come, first served

wicker park >  **e19**

Mana Food Bar embodies the very best of what vegetarianism can be. You'll find no tofurkey here, nor veggie ribs or fake steak. *Mana* shows off vegetables as vegetables—with seductive dishes like mushroom sliders and Thai pineapple salad. These are all foods that might make you wonder why you ever threw a fit about eating your veggies when you were little (or last week, for that matter). Too all the hearty meat eaters out there (Hello Chicago!), come here and just tell me that you're lacking for anything. I dare you.

imbibe / devour:
chai plum & nigori sake
cucumber sakerita
chickpeas
red quinoa
thai pineapple salad
bi bim bop
mana slider
sweet potato pancake

45

marigold

modern indian

4832 north broadway avenue. between lawrence and ainslie. red line: lawrence
773.293.4653 www.marigoldrestaurant.com
sun 5 - 9p tue - thu 5:30 - 10p fri - sat 5:30 - 11p

opened in 2006. owners: james dragatsis and sandeep malhotra
$$: all major credit cards accepted
dinner. reservations recommended

uptown >

My husband has been traveling to India on business recently, and this has made him a know-it-all and absolute expert on the cuisine of this entire vast country. With his new-found expertise, he's turned up his nose at a couple of Indian spots in town. When I brought him to *Marigold* I thought he would dismiss it as in-authentic, because of their modern approach. Wrong-o. As we shoveled hot tikka and fresh naan into our mouths, he gave it his official seal of approval. I hate it when he's right, but was secretly happy he was right about *Marigold*.

imbibe / devour:
kingfisher lager
spiked mango lassi
samosas
dahi kabab
corn bhuta & spinach salad
vegetarian thali
tandoori chicken
naan

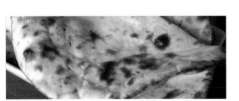

merlo on maple

upscale authentic bolognese

16 west maple street. between dearborn and state. red line: clark
312.335.8200 www.merlochicago.com
daily 5:30p - close

opened in 2001. owners: giampaolo sassi and luisa silvia marani
$$$: all major credit cards accepted
dinner. reservations recommended

gold coast >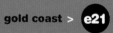

As I decided which eating spots to include in this book, I used the Giampaolo and Silvia litmus test. Though you might think I consider my publisher, friends and family or locals while making up my list, truth be told, I had two people on my mind: the brilliant restauranteurs behind *Merlo on Maple*. Would the places I chose past muster with them? I guess you might ask why I would care. Because *Merlo* to me is perfection. When I sit at the bar here for dinner, the experience is perfect from beginning to end—including, of course, Sylvia's always delicious food.

imbibe / devour:
any cocktail that david the bartender suggests
01 nebbiolo "ghemme" dessilani rsv.
bresaola
insalata di carciofi, funghi & sedano e grana
taglioline paglia e fieno
ravioli di erbette con le noci
tonno rosato
budino di amaretti

mixteco grill

1601 west montrose avenue. corner of ashland. brown line: montrose
773.868.1601
see website for hours

opened in 2008. owners: rosendo neri, rodolfo neri and anselmo ramirez
owner / chef: raul arreola
$$: all major credit cards accepted
dinner. brunch. byo. reservations recommended

lakeview >

When Raul Arreola left *Fonda del Mar* (found in the last edition of this book), I was upset. Where would I indulge my intense cravings for his amazing Mexican cuisine? Angst ensued. And then I learned he had begun a new endeavor in the kitchen at *Mixteco Grill*. Relief flooded through me. But then other members of the Raul fan club starting spreading the good news, and soon *Mixteco* was booked to the gills on the weekends. Angst again. I quickly regrouped and decided I would eat here on Tuesdays. Problem solved. Angst abated. Anna happy and full of Raul's delicious food.

imbibe / devour:
tacos ensenada
sopa azteca
uchepos gratinados
chuleta en manchamanteles
calabacitas rellenas
cochinita pibil
pollo en mole de mango

51

nana

organic breakfast and lunch

3267 south halsted street. corner of 33rd. cta bus: 8
312.929.2486 www.nanaorganic.com
mon - fri 8a - 3p sat - sun 8a - 4p

opened in 2009. owners: omar and chris solis
$-$$. all major credit cards accepted
breakfast. lunch. first come, first served

bridgeport > **e23**

Menus change, dishes come and go, but for all of our sakes, I sincerely hope that the banana hemp pancakes on *Nana's* menu never go away. They are simply more delicious than any pancakes you could make at home, and considering the family affair of Omar, Chris and their mother—Nana—who is always in the kitchen, it isn't surprising that the food here tastes homemade. Add in that everything on *Nana's* menu is organic, as local as can be, you may never eat breakfast or lunch at your own home again.

imbibe / devour:
fresh squeezed beet juice
fresh squeezed granny smith apple juice
liege waffle
banana hemp cakes
mascarpone stuffed french toast
magic mushroom burger
patty melt

nightwood

modern heartland cooking

2119 south halsted street. between 21st and cermak. red line: cermak
312.526.3385 www.nightwoodrestaurant.com
tue - sat 5:30 - 11p brunch sun 9a - 2:30p

opened in 2009. chef / owners: jason hammel and amalea tshilds
$$-$$$: all major credit cards accepted
dinner. brunch. first come, first served

pilsen >

I often fantasize about writing a national *eat.shop guide*. This guide would be an edited selection of my top picks across the country. First on the list from Chicago? *Nightwood*. Once I learned that *Lula Cafe's* owners were opening a new place, I waited anxiously for what seemed like forever. I was sooo excited, I worried that the actual moment might be a disappointment. I'm happy to say that *Nightwood* has not brought me an ounce of disappointment—my only issue is that I just can't seem to get back here often enough.

---

imbibe / devour:
06 alexander valley vineyards cabernet franc
mixed lettuces with croutons, olive oil & vinegar
chilled asparagus soup
raviolo with egg yolk, brown butter & sage
wood grilled cheeseburger with fries & pickle
hand cut pasta with asparagus,
  broccoli leaves, bacon & squash
blueberry sour cream cake

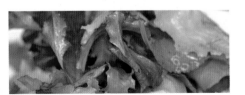

55

old fashioned donuts

just like the name says
11248 south michigan avenue. between 112th and 113th. bus 119: michigan
773.995.7420
mon - sat 6a - 6p

opened in 1972. owner: mr. burritt bulloch
$: visa. mc
treats. first come, first served

roseland >

In the way one prepares for a marathon, I prepared for *Old Fashioned Donuts*. The day before my planned foray here, I ran a few miles, went to yoga, and ate some green veggies. The morning of my trip, I drove 30 minutes to the famed shop, and ordered one of the hefty, much-praised apple fritters. This baby might have weighed as much as a small human one. I'm embarrassed to admit that after my stringent prepping, I couldn't finish the goliath. Obviously I need to take a different training approach and instead stretch out my stomach by eating numerous large training meals. That's the ticket.

imbibe / devour:
doughnuts:
  apple fritter
  texas
  chocolate cake
  glazed
  maple
  jelly-filled
  bow-tie

old oak tap

good beer and good food

2109 west chicago avenue. between hoyne and leavitt. cta bus: 66-chicago
773.772.0406 www.theoldoaktap.com
mon 5p - 2a tue - fri 11a - 2a sat 11a - 3a sun 11a - 2a

opened in 2008. owners: susan and chris ongkiko chef: jason vandergraft
$$: all major credit cards accepted
lunch. dinner. brunch. first come, first served

east village > **e26**

Chicago is a beer town. It always has been. But these days a new sort of beer obsession has evolved—the hops gang have developed a hankering for really good, locally brewed beers, and unusual varieties that come from faraway lands. *Old Oak Tap* is the ideal place to check out out this new scene, as the beer menu is super diverse and it's matched up with some downright great bar food. A pork sampler, you say? Why, yes please. And for you stick-in-the-mud types, and you know who you are, there's an old favorites beer list here just for you, too.

imbibe / devour:
ayinger brau-weisse
magic hat #9
pork sampler
home-made soft pretzels
baja style fish tacos
fat boy pie
grilled sliced flank steak sandwich
deep fried banana stuffed twinkie

olivia's market

a market with everything you want and need
2014 west wabansia avenue. between damen and milwaukee. blue line: damen
773.227.4220 www.oliviasmarket.com
daily 8a - 9p

opened in 2004. owners: bill and joy maheras
$-$$: all major credit cards accepted
grocery. first come, first served

bucktown > **e27**

Baby Red Potatoes
$ .99/lb

Once upon a time, there was a lovely couple in Chicago who opened a lovely neighborhood grocery named *Olivia's Market*. It grew to become everyone's favorite place to shop, even little girls and boys who might get a piece of penny candy on the way out if they were especially good. A trip for groceries became enjoyable, no longer a chore. The owners were glad, the shoppers content and everyone lived happily ever after (author's note: I'm secretly hoping for a sequel, where *Olivia's* opens in my neighborhood. That would be a true fairytale ending).

imbibe / devour:
organic beer
rick's pick's pickles
boar's heads meats
fresh produce
carol's cookies
penny candy
just about anything you need

perman wine selections

802 west washington boulevard. between halsted and green. pink line: clinton-green
312.666.4417 www.permanwine.com
mon - fri noon - 9p sat 11a - 9p or by appointment

opened in 2007. owner: craig perman
$$$: all major credit cards accepted
first come, first served

west loop >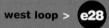

Some people make New Year's resolutions to lose weight, exercise more, drink less. Not Craig Perman. He made a resolution to drink a glass of champagne every day, all year long. He made it six months or so, and then got a bit bubbly-ed out. When some people give up, they walk away from their resolutions completely. In Craig's case—it's not like he could or would lose interest in the grape—he's a veritable encyclopedia of wine knowledge. I suggest your next resolution, and one you should stick to (!) is to visit *Perman Wine Collection* for a bit of vino knowledge.

imbibe / devour:
08 ardilla tempranillo
08 domaine de la pépière "cuvée granit"
07 vietti barbera dl'asti "tre vigne"
06 carm vinho tinto douro
06 aveleda "follies" maria gomes/chardonnay
06 la vis müller-thurgau
06 tenuta di trinoro "le cupole" rossa toscana

province

modern american with spanish and south american influences

161 north jefferson street. between randolph and lake. green pink lines: clinton
312.669.9900 www.provincerestaurant.com
mon - thu 11:30a - 10:30p fri 11:30a - 11:30p sat 5 - 11:30p

opened in 2008. chef / owner: randy zweiban
$$-$$$: all major credit cards accepted
lunch. dinner. reservations recommended

west loop >  **e29**

Living a green lifestyle in the big city can be challenging, though there are some helpful things that come with the territory: using public transit, walking, living in small apartments that are like 1/2 of a carbon footprint. Composting from a high-rise is doable, but harder. Another way to be eco friendly in Chicago? Eat at *Province*. Housed in a LEED-certified city building (check), a few paces from the El (double check), a chef that is serving gorgeous food that covers all the important eco bases: locally sourced, organic and seasonal. See, this eco thing is not that hard after all.

imbibe / devour:
07 altos las hormigas malbec mendoza
yellow moon cocktail
house smoked sable ceviche
artichokes & romanesco salad with serrano ham
farm raised shrimp & anson mills organic grits
slow roasted gunthorp farms pork ropa vieja
chimichurri rubbed flatiron steak
chocolate three ways

sarah's candies

chocolate shop and cafe

70 e oak street / 111 n state street. between michigan and rush / between randolph
and washington. red line: clark/division / red line: lake
312.664.6223 www.sarahscandies.com
mon - sat 8a - 6p sun 10a - 6p / mon - sat 10a - 8p sun 11a - 6p

opened in 2005. owner: owner: sarah levy
$: all major credit cards accepted
breakfast. lunch. treats. first come, first served

gold coast / loop > e30

I recently moved out of the Gold Coast, and while I'm loving my new digs, I'm bemoaning the fact that I am no longer a short walk away from *Sarah's Candies*. It's bad news that I can't make a quick run over for a coffee and a few crunchy bunches of royaltines, or a slab of chunky rocky road, which both require serious will power to stop devouring. But the good news is that since my walk has now more than tripled, I am justified in eating a chocolate-covered marshmallow or perhaps a peanut butter s'more, or even better, both!

imbibe / devour:
intelligentsia coffee
chai tea latte
carrot cream cheese muffin
royaltines
mom's fudge brownie
toffee sugar cookie
chocolate delights
chocolate covered marshmallows

sepia

inventive american cuisine

123 north jefferson street. between randolph and washington. green line: clinton
312.441.1920 www.sepiachicago.com
see website for hours

opened in 2007. owner: emmanuel nony chef: andrew zimmerman
$$-$$$: all major credit cards accepted
lunch. dinner. reservations recommended

west loop > **e31**

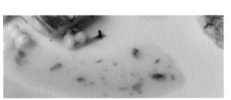

I like to plan. I've never met a reservation, calendar or list I didn't like. On occasion though, I like to break free from my mental tidiness and embrace a *que sera, sera* attitude. On this rare occasion, I like to pop into *Sepia*, grab a seat at the bar, and kick back with a gorgeous cocktail and something mouth-watering from the menu. Sure I could make a reservation, which would be the smart thing to do to ensure a table here, but something about *Sepia* inspires me to be a bit more daring. I suggest though that you put *Sepia* on your list...

imbibe / devour:
cognac et framboise cocktail
jalisco kiss cocktail
lamb shoulder, camelized onions & olives
charred baby octopus
seared sea scallops with sunchoke
duck fat fried potatoes
flat iron steak with knob onions
free form pecan honey phyllo tart

simone's

a cool neighborhood place

960 west 18th street. corner of morgan. orange line: halsted
312.666.8601 www.simonesbar.com
mon - fri 11:30a - 2a sat 11:30a - 3a

opened in 2009. owners: russ and desiree grant and michael noone
chefs: ruth lipsky and jamie lopez
$$: all major credit cards accepted
lunch. dinner. brunch. first come, first served

pilsen > e32

What does it mean to you when you hear somebody say a restaurant is a "great neighborhood place." My translation: the restaurant is somewhat mediocre—good enough for those that are close by, but not good enough to go out of your way to go to. Then there's *Simone's*. Guess what? It's a great neighborhood place. But let me be clear. I'm not saying it's good just for Pilsen; it's good enough to get in your car in Andersonville and come over here. Maybe you'll love it so much here, you'll make *Simone's* your favorite place of the 'hood known as Chicago.

imbibe / devour:
metropolitan flywheel lager
bear republic racer
housemade tomato soup
tempura vegetables
monte cristo sandwich
black bean & banana empanada
simone's pizza
hot fudge ice cream

smoque bbq

destination barbeque

3800 north pulaski road. corner of grace. blue line: irving park
773.545.7427 www.smoquebbq.com
tue - thu 11a - 9p fri - sat 11a - 10p sun 11a - 9p

opened in 2006. owners: al sherman, mike mcdermott and chris hendrickson
chef / owner: barry sorkin
$-$$: all major credit cards accepted
lunch. dinner. byo. first come, first served

irving park > **e33**

On a few select summer days, my husband will set his alarm fo 5 a.m. to pull himself out of bed to begin a marathon day of smoking pork shoulders and ribs for a smoky, barbeque feast. It's delicious, don't get me wrong, but it's a LOT of work. I'm pretty thrilled that we have *Smoque* as a place where we can get pulled pork and ribs when Shawn doesn't have all day to tend a smoker. Though my husband will likely continue his smoking ritual every year, I will continue my ritual to eat as often as possible at *Smoque*.

imbibe / devour:
sweet tea
rootbeer
brisket
pulled pork sandwich
baby back ribs
fries
baked beans
peach cobbler

southport grocery and café

upscale grocery and café

3552 north southport avenue. between addison and cornelia. brown line: southport
773.665.0100 www.southportgrocery.com
mon - fri 7a - 4p sat 8a - 5p sun 8a - 4p

opened in 2003. chef / owner: lisa santos
$$: all major credit cards accepted
breakfast. lunch. first come, first served

lakeview >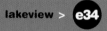

Here's the proof that *Southport Grocery* makes drool-worthy food: the place is swarming with pregnant women. Though the bun in the oven crowd sometimes has some off-kilter cravings, most of the time they want satisfying, healthy, homey food. This pretty much sums up *Southport.* And I probably don't even need to mention their famous cupcake, which at this point probably has a city holiday named after it, though I will mention the cupcake pancakes, a downright genius idea. You know you are going to wake up tomorrow craving some of those.

imbibe / devour:
lavender lemon mimosa
bloody mary
stuffed french toast
grilled coffee cake
the cupcake pancakes
chocolate toffee scone
tuna melt
grilled brie

takashi

french-american meets japanese

1952 north damen avenue. between armitage and homer. blue line: damen
773.772.6170 www.takashichicago.com
tue - thu 5:30 - 10p fri - sat 5 - 10:30p sun 11a - 3p, 5 - 9:30p

opened in 2007. chef / owner: takashi yagihashi
$$-$$$: all major credit cards accepted
dinner. sunday noodle lunch. reservations recommended

bucktown > **e35**

You might think that getting a best new restaurant of the year award might go to a chef's head. Not Takashi's. When I came here to take pictures, a year after Chicago magazine gave him this honor, he was still racing around like a newbie chef—taking reservations, preparing food for the photos, even mixing me a drink—all the while staying jovial as all get out. He said, smiling, "You own your own restaurant, you have to do everything!" No ego at work here. And did I mention his food is out of this world?

imbibe / devour:
blood orange martini
lost in translation cocktail
soy cured scottish salmon
spring roll
sashimi plate
grilled marinated beef short ribs
roasted alaskan halibut
dark chocolate cremeux

taxim

greek cuisine

1558 north milwaukee avenue. between north and honore. blue line: damen
773.252.1558 www.taximchicago.com
see website for hours

opened in 2009. chef / owner: david schneider
$$-$$$: all major credit cards accepted
dinner. reservations recommended

wicker park > **e36**

When I think about where to eat, I often think about it in seasonal terms. There are certain spots I head to when it's frigid outside, so I can warm up with hearty food—I put Belgian, German and French places in this category. Then there's the other side of the weather report for eating, places where the food is refreshing and light—think sushi. What do I feel like in any weather? *Taxim*. This stellar Greek restaurant works for me year round, with food that seems to work with any season.

imbibe / devour:
06 domaine skouras viognier
05 domain karydas xinomavro
piperies
faki
melitzanosalata
rampopita
arnaki me kapnisto pligouri
duck gyro

the bluebird

wine, beer and food from all over the country

1749 north damen avenue. between bloomingdale and wabansia. blue line: damen
773.486.2473 www.bluebirdchicago.com
mon - fri 5p - 2a sat 5p - 3a sun 5p - 2a

opened in 2007. owners: tom macdonald and janan asfour
$$: all major credit cards accepted
dinner. first come, first served

bucktown > **e37**

Beers can have a lot of different and unusual undernotes: raisin, plum, coffee, chocolate. Whatever your beer palette can imagine will be found in one or more of the beers on the list at *The Bluebird*. The menu here is pages long, featuring ales and lagers from all over the world that will satisfy every taste. If you think the beer decision-making process is too tough, then start with some of the fantastic food, where you can't go wrong. And if you discover a beer with a curry undernote, let me know—that sounds interesting.

imbibe / devour:
le merle saison
dorothy goodbody's stout
helles schlenkerla lagerbier
serrano ham, manchego & egg flatbread
mac & cheese gratin
grilled kassler-style pork chop
chocolate dipped figs & dates stuffed with
    marcona almonds

the coffee studio

5628 north clark street. corner of olive. red line: bryn mawr
773.271.7881 www.thecoffeestudio.com
daily 6:30a - 9p

opened in 2007. owners: miguel and lee corrina cano
$: all major credit cards accepted
breakfast. lunch. coffee / tea. first come, first served

andersonville >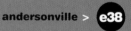

Though the thought of sitting at a coffee shop working or reading sounds appealing, more often than not the atmosphere is not quite right. I do admit I'm a bit like Goldilocks when it comes to my coffee shop preferences, but I have found one that works for me in all regards: *The Coffee Studio*. This is the brightest and most lovely spot I could imagine for enjoying a morning cup, and its apt use of the word "studio" furthers the point that a bunch of artisans are making the coffee here. Even the porridge (i.e. a yummy little cup of steamed milk oatmeal), is juuuust riiight.

imbibe / devour:
fresh, locally roasted cup of intelligentsia
cafe au lait
red eye
chai latter
frozen mocha
oatmeal & milk
cinnamon raisin oatmeal
chocolate chip cookie

the depot american diner

a classic diner

5840 west roosevelt road. between mayfield and monitor. blue line: austin
773.261.8422
mon - sat 6a - 10p sun 6a - 8p

opened in 1997. owners: robert nava and annamarie fillmore nava
$: visa. mc
breakfast. lunch. dinner. first come, first served

austin >

We all have responsibilities that we can't ignore. Mine is to go to *The Depot American Diner* and try out every freshly made carbohydrate on the menu. While everyone is busy watching their carb consumption, calorie counting and exercising, I will take on the grueling task of carbo testing. If you do decide to take a break from your responsibilities and make a trip here, I'd recommend the biscuits and gravy, made-to-order doughnuts, French toast and perhaps the pear pancakes, too. Just be forewarned: this is hard work, and I'd hate for anyone (my boss) to think otherwise.

imbibe / devour:
egg cream
phosphate
apple pancakes
french toast
corn beef hash & eggs
reuben
hamburger
blue plate specials

the fish guy market

fish monger

4423 north elston avenue. between montrose and keeler. cta bus 53-pulaski
773.283.7400 www.fishguy.com
mon - sat 10a - 6p

opened in 1998. owner: bill dugan
$$: all major credit cards accepted
lunch. weekly wellfleet dinner. market. classes. first come, first served

albany park > **e40**

There is much to tell you about *The Fish Guy Market* and the fish guy himself, Bill Dugan, in such a tiny space—but I'm going to go for it. First, come here for lunch to get insanely yummy fish tacos and lobster rolls. Second, come here for the once-weekly dinner on Friday called *Wellfleet*, and indulge in a luxurious prix fixe, seafood laden meal. Third and most importantly, come here to buy fresh, sustainably harvested seafood. So there's many an option to chose from, but if I were you, I would sign on for the whole *Fish Guy* experience: lunch, dinner and some seafood to take home with you.

imbibe / devour:
colassal king crab legs
sushi grade bluefin tuna
wellfleet oysters
golden trout
lunch:
  fish tacos
  lobster roll
  clamwich

the whistler

sublime, laid-back cocktail bar

2421 north milwaukee avenue. between fullerton and richmond blue line: california
773.227.3530 www.whistlerchicago.com
see website for hours

opened in 2008. owners: billy helmkamp and robert brenner
$$: all major credit cards accepted
bar. first come, first served

logan square > e41

I do not like fussy, girly, sweetened, silly-looking cocktails. If I find an umbrella, a small plastic monkey or a neon stir stick in my drink I get surly. What I do love is a precisely executed, creatively crafted cocktail. What do I mean by this? A classy glass (no more martini glasses, please!), nice big ice cubes, carefully chosen spirits and house-made syrups and infusions. Hence my fondness for *The Whistler*. The cocktails are so good here (and never silly), and the place so understatedly cool, you might find an unexpected line out the door of its unexpected location.

imbibe / devour:
cocktails:
  dark & stormy
  the old square
  pinga
beer:
  three floyds
  great lakes
  bells

tocco

mod italian restaurant

1266 north milwaukee avenue. between ashland and paulina. blue line: division
773.687.8895 www.toccochicago.com
see website for hours

opened in 2009. chef / owner: bruno abate
$$-$$$: all major credit cards accepted
dinner. brunch. reservations recommended

wicker park > **e42**

I just got the newest iPhone, and here's what I've learned so far: anything one needs, there's an app for it. There have been days when just one touch to the screen is all I have needed to put my world right. There are realistic downsides to this wonder device though: it won't do my work for me, and I haven't found an app to make me food like *Tocco's*. Though its mod, shiny white interior feels a bit like an Apple product, this shiny spot specializes in fresh made pasta and brick oven pizzas. I suspect you'll be so content eating here, you might even put down your iPhone (hint hint).

imbibe / devour:
bresaola
piccola caprese
spaghetti aglio e olio
spaghetti carbonara
margherita pizza
quattro stagioni pizza
torta di mele

urbanbelly

modern dumpling house

3053 north california avenue. between nelson and barry. blue line: california
773.583.0500 www.urbanbellychicago.com
tue - sun 11a - 9p

opened in 2008. chef / owner: bill kim
$$: all major credit cards accepted
lunch. dinner. byo. first come, first served

avondale >

Pssst. Hey you. Keep your voice down. I've got a secret. One of the best meals to be had in this city these days is at *Urban Belly*. Why am I whispering? Because last time I checked, there weren't any crazy lines of foodies snaking out the door that have been spotted at various other places in town of late. So if you can keep this our secret, we will be able to get in here and grab a seat at one of the communal tables without an hour long wait. Just be careful—don't sit too close to your tablemates, lest they be tempted to snag one of your precious dumplings or a short rib. Heathens.

imbibe / devour:
asian squash & bacon dumplings
pork & cilantro dumplings
organic pea shoots & thai basil rice
short rib & scallion rice
urbanbelly ramen
rice cake noodles
wrinkle beans
chinese eggplant with thai basil

XOCO

tortas, churros and chocolate

449 north clark street. corner of illinois. brown / purple lines: merchandise mart
www.xocochicago.com
tue - sat 7a - 10p

opened in 2009. chef / owner: rick bayless
$-$$: all major credit cards accepted
breakfast. lunch. dinner. carry out. first come, first served

river north > 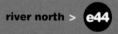 **e44**

I am the youngest of three sisters, so when *Xoco*, meaning "little sister" opened recently as the third *Frontera* sibling (*Topolobampo* and *Frontera Grill* being the others), I had an immediate affinity for it—nevermind that I would be attracted to just about any place that Rick Bayless opened. Just as there is always a bit of competition between siblings, it's hard to pick which of this trio I love the most with their different charms, but *Xoco's* freshly ground chocolate and hot churros make me think that the little sister has leaped to the top of my list. Aren't little sisters the best?

imbibe / devour:
ultra: chocolate shot & whole milk
chocolate café con leche
churros
mexican vanilla-sour cream coffeecake
ahogada torta
choriqueso torta
xoco salad
shortrib red chile soup

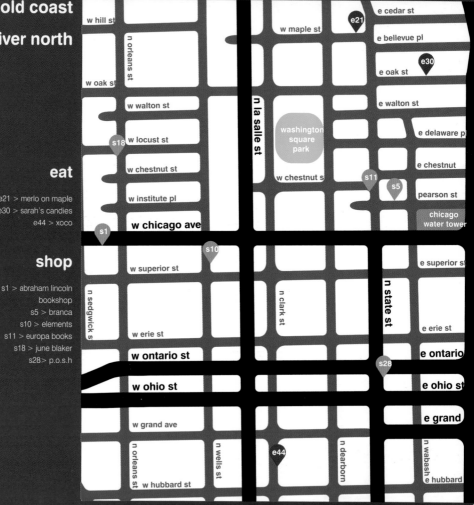

- **gold coast**
- **river north**

eat

e21 > merlo on maple
e30 > sarah's candies
e44 > xoco

shop

s1 > abraham lincoln
bookshop
s5 > branca
s10 > elements
s11 > europa books
s18 > june blaker
s28> p.o.s.h

w hill st
w oak st
n orleans st
w walton st
w locust st
w chestnut st
w institute pl
w chicago ave
w superior st
n sedgwick s
w erie st
w ontario st
w ohio st
w grand ave
n orleans st
w hubbard st
n wells st
n clark st

w maple st
n la salle st
washington square park
w chistnut s
n dearborn
e44

e cedar st
e21
e bellevue pl
e30
e oak st
e walton st
e delaware p
e chestnut
s11
s5
pearson st
chicago water tower
e superior st
n state st
e erie st
e ontario
s28
e ohio st
e grand
n wabash
e hubbard

n lake shore dr
n michigan ave

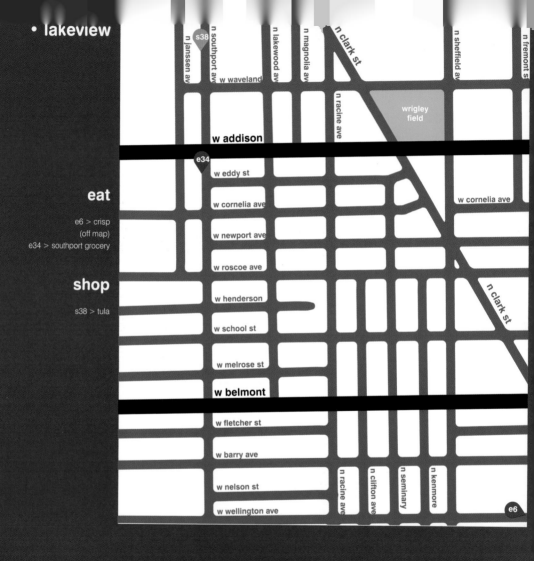

• lakeview

eat

e6 > crisp
(off map)
e34 > southport grocery

shop

s38 > tula

s38
n janssen av
n southport ave
w waveland
n lakewood ave
n magnolia ave
n clark st
n racine ave
wrigley field
n sheffield av
n fremont s

w addison

e34
w eddy st
w cornelia ave
w newport ave
w roscoe ave
w henderson
w school st
w melrose st
w belmont

w cornelia ave

n clark st

w fletcher st
w barry ave
w nelson st
w wellington ave

n racine ave
n clifton ave
n seminary
n kenmore

e6

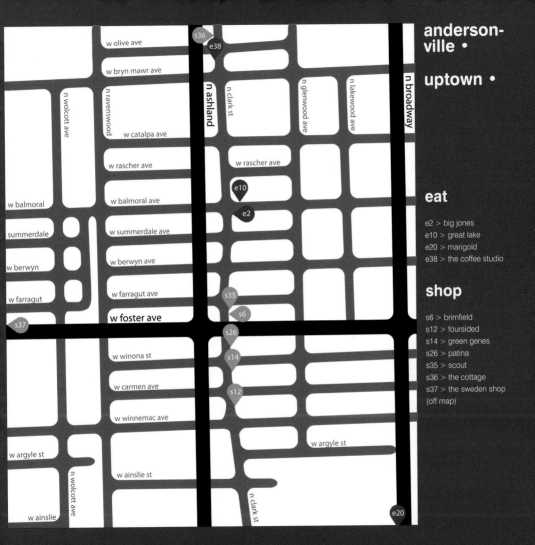

anderson-ville •

uptown •

eat

e2 > big jones
e10 > great lake
e20 > marigold
e38 > the coffee studio

shop

s6 > brimfield
s12 > foursided
s14 > green genes
s26 > patina
s35 > scout
s36 > the cottage
s37 > the sweden shop
(off map)

- **lincoln square**
- **north center**

eat

e14 > kan pou
e22 > mixteco grill

shop

s21 > merz apothecary
s30 > quake toys

w giddings st
w leland ave
w eastwood ave
w wilson ave
w sunnyside ave
welles park
w montrose ave
w pensacola ave
w cullom ave
w berteau
w wamer ave
w belle plaine
w cuyler ave

n damen ave
n winchester
n wolcott ave
n ravenswood
n hermitage
n paulina st
n ashland
n claremont
n leavitt st
n winchester
n oakley ave
n bell ave
n lincoln ave
n western

s21
s30
e22
e14

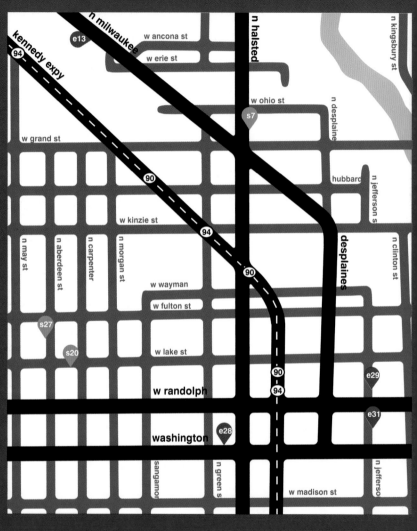

- river west
- west loop

eat

e13 > juicy wine co.
e28 > perman wine selections
e29 > province
e31 > sepia

shop

s7 > caste
s20 > koros
s27 > pivot

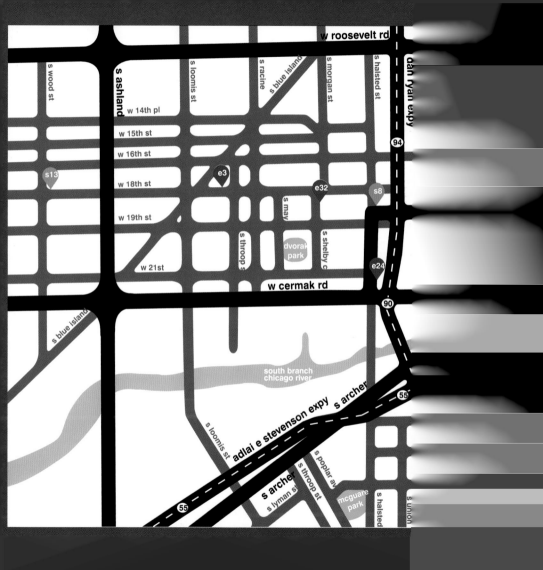

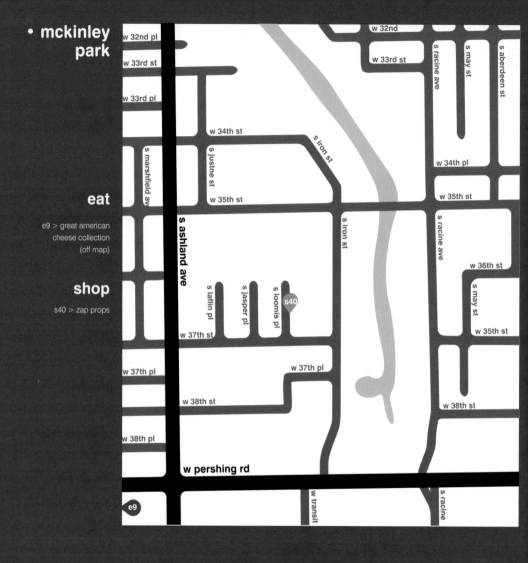

• mckinley park

eat

e9 > great american
cheese collection
(off map)

shop

s40 > zap props

notes

abraham lincoln book shop, inc.

lincoln, civil war and presidential book shop

357 west chicago avenue. between orleans and sedgwick. brown line: chicago
312.944.3085 www.alincolnbookshop.com
mon - wed 9a - 5p thu 9a - 7p fri 9a - 5p sat 10a - 4p

opened in 1938. owner: daniel weinberg
visa. mc.
online shopping

river north >

Pretty soon, they'll probably start calling Illinois, the "Land of Obama." But until then, Abe's still got seniority here, and if you need to know anything about him, this is the place to come. Okay, so he isn't the sole subject of the *Abraham Lincoln Book Shop*, you can find items that involve some of his fellow presidents and a war or two—but for the most part, Abe's the main attraction. Browse a little, learn a little, sight-see (some incredible historical documents hang on the walls here) and feel pride for one of our greatest presidents.

covet:
every lincoln history book you could imagine
limited edition set of sandburg's lincoln
a wax impression from lincoln's original
    presidential seal
1863 map of battle of gettsyburg
civil war history books
washington statuette
original handout at gettysburg address

apartment number 9

smart men's shop

1804 north damen avenue. between churchill and wabansia. blue line: damen
773.395.2999 www.apartmentnumber9.com
mon - fri 11a - 7p sat 11a - 6p sun noon - 5p

opened in 2001. owners: sarah and amy blessing
all major credit cards accepted

bucktown >  s02

"*Apartment Number 9*? Your sisters own that store?! Wow." I hear this all the time from new acquaintences, other store owners, total strangers. I've come to realize that my two older sisters have, over the past eight years, developed quite a name for themselves. It's good to get outside confirmation, otherwise I might start to suspect that my conviction that this is the best men's store in the city, maybe the country... maybe the whole darn world—is a little biased. But I love my sisters and I love *Apartment Number 9.*

covet:
dries van noten
margiela
relwen
band of outsiders
paul smith
steven alan
billy reid
jack spade

asrai garden

an exquisite floral store

1935 west north avenue. between damen and wood. blue line: damen
773.782.0680 www.asraigarden.com
mon - sat 10 a- 7p sun noon - 4p

opened in 1999. owner: elizabeth cronin
all major credit cards accepted
deliveries. weddings. events

wicker park > **s03**

I recently decided that some of the best gifts are ones that disappear quickly: wine, homemade baked goods and flowers. These are all items that take up no permanent space and add no extra clutter. That's why I like to give (and even better, receive) arrangements from *Asrai Garden*. Though there is one small problem. I never want *Asrai's* flowers to go away. Someone once gave me a sweet little bouquet from here that I adored. It sat in my room for weeks past its prime because I was so sad to part with it. The only solution is to treat yourself and your friends at *Asrai* regularly.

covet:
flowers!!
herbs de cèment
john derian
laura zindel
patch nyc
tamar mogendorf
santa maria novella
caskata

bari zaki studio

a book-maker's studio

2119 west roscoe street. between hamilton and hoyne. brown line: addison
773.294.7766 www.barizaki.com
mon - fri 11a - 7ish sat - sun by apointment

opened in 1988. owner: bari zaki
visa. mc
custom orders/design

roscoe village > s04

As I toured *Bari Zaki's* immaculately kept studio, I found my mind wandering to the 'Spoonful of Sugar' scene from Mary Poppins. Bari certainly understands that "in every job that must be done, there is an element of fun." As I perused the custom books and keepsake boxes, I realized that what I really wanted was for Bari to organize my entire life. Unfortunately that isn't a service she offers, so I'll have to be content with some one-of-a-kind note cards or a hand bound book. Whatever you choose here, it will be a lark, a spree, it's very clear to see!

covet:
custom books
custom boxes
envelopes made with vintage
   correspondence & stamps
letterprecious labels
tape escape dots
japanese style journals
noteworthy miscellany

branca

incredible interior design shop

17 east pearson street. between state and wabash. red line: chicago
312.787.1017 www.branca.com
tue - sat 10a - 6p

opened in 2008. owner: alessandra branca
all major credit cards accepted

gold coast > **s05**

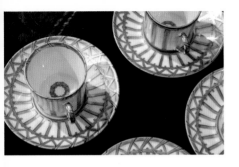

If you're an interior design mag junkie like me, you've no doubt come across spreads on houses where Alessandra Branca has designed the interior. Her work is jaw-droppingly, out-of-this-world stunning. I tend to devour these pages, holding them up to my nose so I can see each glorious detail. I want to crawl inside the pages to touch the fabrics and sit on the furniture. While I've never toured one of these fantasy houses, I can certainly tour her store, *Branca*. Even taking home just a little something from here makes me feel like I have a bit of Alessandra's magic in my own home.

covet:
gold agenda book
etched garnet lowball glasses
gilt faux bois candleholder
log stool with gold leaf finish
blue ikat dinner placemats
shagreen tray
natural pine candlesticks
porcelain charger with geometric maps

121

brimfield

vintage plaids and home accessories
5219 north clark street. between farragut and foster. red line: berwyn
312.593.6415
call store for hours

opened in 2009. owner: julie fernstrom
all major credit cards accepted

andersonville > 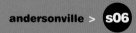 s06

As I was shooting pictures of *Scout* for this book, I noticed some activity next door. Another vintage home store, I thought—would it compete with *Scout*? A week later when *Brimfield* opened, I came back to explore. Alas, no competition here, but something much better—a store that is a great complement to *Scout* and a fantastic addition to the neighborhood. *Brimfield* is all about English country chic and you'll find plaids a-plenty (Brimfield being the most desirable pattern). And while you are exploring Andersonville, make sure to visit Julie's other store, *The Cottage*.

covet:
plaid blankets
vintage scotch tape tins
pull-down map of the united states
metal buckets
wooden ladders
picnic basket
plaid thermos
quilts

caste

handmade furniture, art and objects
521 north halsted street. between ohio and grand. blue line: grand
312.432.0717 www.castedesign.us
tue - fri 11a - 6p sat 11a - 5p

opened in 2007. owners: brad rowley and ty best
all major credit cards accepted

river west >

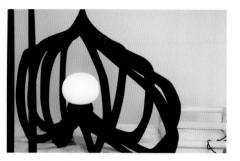

Caste has me fantasizing about leaving Chicago. I imagine this store as the modern version of a Western ranch house, and it makes me dream of moving out west to live a rancher's life, and of course I will need to take this entire store with me to fulfill the vision. While I figure out the details for this plan, I think I'll start selling my possessions to make way for the lights, benches and amazing pieces here that are created from wood sourced in Montana, and designed by Ty. So goodbye big city, and hello to life on the range—that is if it involves pieces from *Caste*.

covet:
handmade furniture, art & objects:
  stools
  candleholders
  trays
  birds
  lights
  tables

deliciously vintage

vintage for women

1747 south halsted street. between 17th and 18th. orange line: halsted
312.733.0407 www.dvchicago.com
tue - sat noon - 7p sun by appointment

opened in 2009. owners: law roach and siobhan strong
all major credit cards accepted

pilsen >

While raving recently about Pilsen, I've heard a few grumbles from people about it being too far to travel. Come on! Too far is Detroit... Pilsen and *Deliciously Vintage* are just a couple of miles away from wherever you are in Chicago. Think about it. All of the serious legwork is being done here by Law and Siobhan, as they are constantly on the prowl to fill their vintage store with primo finds. This means you can skip the trips to suburban estate sales and know they are doing the traveling for you. I bet you are now thinking that *Deliciously Vintage* is just a short jaunt away.

covet:
vintage:
  ralph lauren
  fendi
  christian dior
  halsten
  clutches
  $5 rack

dovetail

vintage for men, women and home

1452 west chicago avenue. between greenview and bishop. cta bus: 66-chicago
312.243.3100 www.dovetailchicago.com
wed - fri 1 - 8p sat 11a - 8p sun 10a - 4p

opened in 2008. owners: jennifer clower and julie ghatan
all major credit cards accepted

noble square >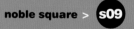

I recently decided to try to stop multitasking. Then I came to *Dovetail*, where Jennifer and Julie take this sometimes dubious skill to a brilliant new level. They both maintain other jobs (Jennifer is co-owner of *Lustre Skin Boutique*), and yet somehow they dug out the time and creative energy to open this adorable shop filled with extremely desirable vintage pieces for guys and gals. They even have the occasional art opening and party at the store. How do they find the time? They are multitasking prodigies, I decided. Maybe doing two things at once really is the answer.

covet:
vintage:
  belts
  bangles
  bags
  rings
  shoes
  ties
  dresses

elements

741 north wells street. between superior and chicago. brown line: chicago
312.642.6574 www.elementschicago.com
mon - sat 10a - 6p sun 11a - 5p

opened in 1987. owners: toby glickman and jeannine dal pra
all major credit cards accepted
online shopping. registries

river north > **s10**

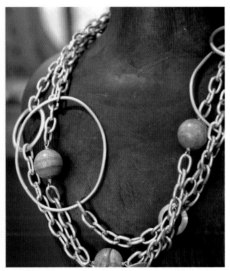

Ages ago, *Elements* first opened on Wells. Then they moved to Oak, which is where I became aware of them. It was a beautiful place that I would gaze into, but it seemed to call out to a more moneyed and mature audience. Then *Elements* moved back to Wells last year, and it went through a total transformation. Though it maintained its previous beauty, it also became, dare I say, edgier—and with the addition of a coffee bar—I became besotted. Now this is one of my go to places to get gifts for friends and family of any age. And I sometimes gift myself a little something.

covet:
nymphen burg plates
star of david rosaries
craft design scissors
apostrophe bookends
zambos & siega woven clutch
jaime joseph jewelry
ted muehling candlesticks
abahna soaps & bath oil

131

europa books

foreign language bookstore

832 north state street. between chestnut and pearson. red line: chicago
312.335.9677 www.schoenhofs.com
mon - sat 10a - 7p sun 10a - 6p

opened in 1992
all major credit cards accepted
online shopping

gold coast > **s11**

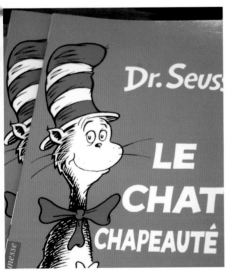

I grew up reading Tin Tin in French, Beatrix Potter in German, and other children's classics in foreign languages, brought home by my parents from their faraway travels. Though I couldn't understand these languages at the time, it didn't change how much I loved the books and it lit a flame in me to learn the languages. *Europa Books* is now my source for buying children's books in foreign languages (though they stock all kinds of books), and where I stock up on hard-to-find international mags. *Domo arigato* Europa.

covet:
foreign language:
  dictionaries
  magazines
  literature
babar nell'isola
le petit prince
coco fahrt rad
tin tin in any language

foursided

more than just a frame shop

a: 5061 north clark street. corner of carmen. red line: argyle
l: 2939 north broadway avenue. between wellington and oakdale
brown / purple lines: wellington
a: 773.506.8300 / l: 773.248.1960 www.foursided.com
mon - sat 11a - 7p sun 11a - 5p

opened in 2006. owners: todd mack and gino pinto
all major credit cards accepted
custom services

andersonville / lakeview > **s12**

I have a friend, Katie, who is a genius at framing her art in the least expected ways, and then hanging it. I, on the other hand, buy art, and then let it sit, agonizing over which frame to use, and where to hang the piece. Argh. I have found a partial solution to this problem: *Foursided*. Not only are they expert framers here, but take a look around this place, Todd and Gino have a great eye for style—this place is as much great gift store and gallery as framer. Now I just need to find someone to do the hanging… Katie, are you available?

covet:
vintage flash cards
old maps & prints
wood alphabet blocks
framing:
  floating frames
  special mat design
  memory boxes
twosided (foursided's sister store)

135

golden age

a gallery of sorts

1744 west 18th street. between wood and paulina. pink line: 18th street
312.850.2574 www.shopgoldenage.com
wed - sun noon - 6p

opened in 2007. owners: marco kane and martine syms
all major credit cards accepted
online shopping

pilsen > **s13**

XIU XIU
THE POLAROID PROJECT

My memories of summer camp focus on the arts and crafts I did (waterskiing water wedgies are less enjoyable reminiscences). I enjoyed a hodge podge of activites: hand-tooling leather keychains, throwing pots, braiding lanyards. *Golden Age* reminds me of those summer days, except the crafts here are exquisitely made. And if you haven't had a creative experience since your own days at summer camp, *Golden Age* may well inspire you to tap back into your artistic side or if that's out of reach, just buy something here and hopethe artistic expression will rub off on you.

covet:
lulu geo necklace
a-z collection mason bag
slow and steady wins the race clear circle glasses
souvenir patchwork shirt
sighn - its ok
david horvitz tour clouds poster
peter sutherland muddy treads book
the fluxus coloring book

green genes

eco goods for babes and tots

5111 north clark street. between winona and carmen. red line: argyle
773.944.9250 www.green-genes.com
see website for hours

opened in 2008. owners: heather muenstermann and christina isperduli
all major credit cards accepted
online shopping

andersonville >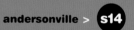

We can't pick and choose which genes our kids will inherit, but we can show them how to live a life that's kind to this planet. At *Green Genes*, Heather and Christina make eco-friendliness fun for both adults and kids. Start your babes off on the right (green) foot with organic onesies and wash them with Erbaviva natural soap, and maybe by the time they're in high school they'll be sipping out of their aluminum bottles saying, "tell us the story again of how you used to drink out of throw-away plastic water bottles."

covet:
cheekeyes wooden animals
clementine art kits
green toys gardening kit
chapter one organic diapers
recycled wool strolled blanket
speesies clothing
sckoon clothing
erbaviva

greer

my favorite stationery store

1657 north wells street. corner of eugenie. brown / purple lines: sedgwick
312.337.8000 www.greerchicago.com
mon - fri 11a - 6:30p sat 11a - 6p

opened in 2005. owner: chandra greer
all major credit cards accepted
online shopping

old town > **s15**

I've tried. I really have. But it's just not possible. I can't show you how great this store is with just five small photographs. Sure I can give you a sense of *Greer*, but you have to actually come here, touch things, look closely, and walk around and around and around, each new circle revealing desirable items that you didn't notice on the first circle. To try to sum up *Greer* in just five measly shots, like I said, is impossible. I'm thinking I need a full book to show the brilliance and beauty of this special stationery boutique. Maybe I can get Kaie to publish it for me.

covet:
greer civilettes portable thank you notes
yellow caran d'ache office ballpoint
angela adams address book
vintage 1966 bluebook of telephone numbers
mateo ilasco everything
set editions postcards
soolip calendar
art school girl heart keys

habit

a design collective

1951 west division street. between damen and winchester. blue line: division
773.342.0093 www.habitchicago.com
tue - sat 11a - 7p sun noon - 5p

opened in 2005. owner: lindsey boland
all major credit cards accepted
online shopping

wicker park > **s16**

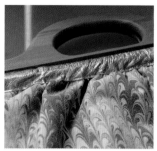

Having a reputation as a nit picky organizer and clearer-outter, I've been enlisted by several friends and family to help clean out closets. I find the trap that stale wardrobes most often fall into is habit. Habit meaning, same old/same old, this is comfortable, that is familiar. If you really want to clear things out and sharpen your style, head to your new *Habit*. Everything is fresh and exciting here, and Lindsey's roundup of local and indie designers ensures that you will soon have new favorites that you won't want to part with—as pieces from here are bound to survive future closet clear-outs for sure.

covet:
suzabelle
kelly lane
cinderloop
filly
emma carroll etc.
ruth zelanski
sinew
salt water sandals

hadley

smart design for smart babies

1205 west webster avenue. between racine and magnolia. purple / red lines: fullerton
773.883.0077 www.hadleybaby.com
tue - fri 11a - 7p sat 11a - 5p sun 11a - 4p

opened in 2007. owners: dean and maribeth marshall
all major credit cards accepted
online shopping. registries

lincoln park > s17

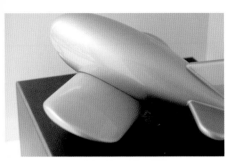

Do you ever wonder what great creative minds like Frank Lloyd Wright or Henry Moore played with when they were babies or what type of crib they slept in? Do you speculate about what could have happened if they had Alexander Calder pull toys or Kapla building blocks at their disposal? We'll never know, but you can surround your mini Matisse with great design at an early age with cool stuff from *Hadley*, where you'll not only find toys, but kid's essentials like high chairs and strollers. Kids and creativity go hand-in-hand, and *Hadley* is there to help!

covet:
playsam planes
netto collection cribs
cariboo folding bassinet
plan toys dancing alligator
vilac calder kangaroo
bloom loft highchair
dwellstudio hooded towel
netto polar bear rocker

june blaker

high style novelty items, jewelry and curiosities
870 north orleans street. between oak and chicago. brown line: chicago
312.751.9220 www.juneblaker.com
tue - sat noon - 5p

opened in 2007. owner: june blaker
all major credit cards accepted

river north >

Ever since June Blaker first saw "Blade Runner," she dreamed of and searched for the glowing umbrellas—a lit up shaft with black hood—seen in the movie. Decades later, she found them, and they became one of the quirky items she stocks at her eponymous store *June Blaker*. Recently, however, the umbrella company folded, and her hunt began anew. This is the persistence of June—and it shows in everything here. Whereas there's an incredible eclecticism on display, nothing is random. You know that June has carefully hand-picked everything right down to the smallest mounted butterfly.

covet:
batucada bracelets
samantha goldberg jewelry
lumen candles
redshift leather
commes des garçons wallets
gear part candlesticks
mounted & framed butterflies
gillion carrara lead-crystal rings

kokorokoko

fashions from the '80s, '90s and '00s

1112 north ashland avenue. between division and augusta. blue line: division
773.252.6996 www.koko-rokoko.blogspot.com
mon - sat noon - 8p sat noon - 6p

opened in 2009. owners: ross kelly and sasha hodges
all major credit cards accepted

west town > s19

When I first met Sasha at *Kokorokoko* she was wearing crazily patterned, somehow amazingly flattering, shiny spandex leggings. If there's anybody out there who knows how to wear things like scrunchies and acid wash, it's Sasha—she's the guru of polka dots, shoulder pads, Keds, fanny packs and neon. No late 20th century trends have been overlooked. These are the styles of my youth, so I'm rejoicing that they are experiencing a renaissance. Now, if only I hadn't gotten rid of my parachute pants. Hopefully *Kokorokoko* will have some.

covet:
vests
keds
polka dots
neon
waste packs
shoulder pads
acid-wash denim
scrunchies

koros

cool city style

1039 west lake street. between carpenter and aberdeen. green / pink lines: clinton
312.738.0155 www.shopkoros.com
mon - tue noon - 6p wed - sat 11a - 7p sun noon - 6p

opened in 2005. owner: kristen skordilis
all major credit cards accepted

west loop >  **s20**

Many stores open, and then for the next 2, 5 or 10 years, never seem to switch things up. Sure, the merchandise changes, but what about the place itself? I've found that some of the best women's boutiques in Chicago—*Robin Richman*, *p.45* and *Koros*—keep their shops up-to-date with major, clean-sweep, total makeovers. Kristen recently moved into a new space a few stores down from her old one, and completely updated and sharpened *Koros's* vintage-inspired look. I loved the old place, but I have to say, I love the new one even more.

covet:
hoss
camilla skovgaard
antik batik
birenzweig
sportmax
gary graham
mischen
anlo denim

merz apothecary

4716 north lincoln avenue. between lawrence and leland. brown line: western
111 north state street. first floor in macy's. red line: randolf
773.989.0900 www.smallflower.com
ls: mon - sat 9a - 6p / macy's: daily

opened in 1875. owners: anthony qaiyum, abdul qaiyum, r.ph and michael winter, r.ph
all major credit cards accepted
online shopping

lincoln square > **s21**

Friends, immortality is to be found at *Merz Apothecary*. Half of the store is dedicated to rejuvenating and improving your health, giving you a good chance at eternal life. The other half is dedicated to keeping your skin youthful and beautiful while you are enjoying this newfound eternal life. Who wants to be sticking around forever without well-nourished, glowing skin? Not I. Beyond all the life-altering and beauty-enhancing potions, aids and panaceas that abound in this apothecary, it's just plain ol' good shopping fun to browse the products here.

covet:
smallflower trading almond milk & saffron soap
grether's pastilles
dr. hauschka
herbacin hand cream
suki skincare
klorane dry shampoo
badger stress soother balm
kneipp herbal bath

michael del piero good design

an interior designer's store

1914 north damen avenue. between armitage and cortland. blue line: damen
773.772.3000 www.michaeldelpiero.com
mon by appointment tue - sat 11a - 6p sun noon - 5p

opened in 2008. owner: michael del piero
visa. mc
design services

bucktown >

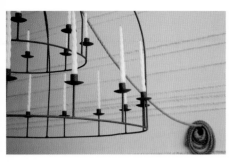

Nothing is as expected at *Michael del Piero Good Design*. The first surprise comes from learning that interior designer and shop owner Michael is in fact a female. Another surprise might be that there are as many treasures here from Chicago-based artists as there are from international talents. Michael's ability at creating the unexpected and striking is found at nearly every little glorious corner here, and you may find yourself forever spoiled for anything considered usual or ordinary after visiting this quite extraordinary place.

covet:
baluchi pillows
industrial oval table
antique african berber bench
lucy slininski lights
mid-century chairs
oversized african vessel
argentinian rugs
oversized boiled wool chairs

optimo hats

custom hat maker

10215 south western avenue. between 103rd and 102nd. metrarail: 103rd
773.238.2999 www.optimohats.com
mon - sat 10a - 6p

opened in 1994. owner: graham thompson
all major credit cards accepted
custom orders

beverly > **s23**

It's hard to find fine craftsman in this country, because they keep getting replaced by machines and conveyer belts. Let me therefore introduce you to *Optimo Hats*. Graham, the owner, is a true craftsman who brings skill, finesse and enormous attention to detail in his hat-making. He uses equipment from the South of France, travels to Ecuador for supplies to make the Montecristi straw hat and sources ribbons in Europe. If all this doesn't make you into a *Optimo* hat-wearer, I don't know what will.

covet:
hats:
   montecristi panama straw
   milan straw
   the manhattan
   the classic fedora
   trilby
   the traveler
   the adventurer

p.45

long-standing women's boutique
1643 north damen avenue. between north and wabansia. blue line: damen
773.862.4523 www.p45.com
mon - sat 11a - 7p sun noon - 5p

opened in 1997. owners: tricia tunstall and judy yin keller
all major credit cards accepted
online shopping

bucktown > **s24**

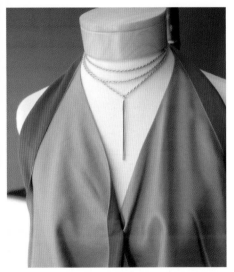

Forgetting all my resolutions to better self and character, I recently started a list of beauty resolutions. On my list: Wear prettier undergarments. Never leave the house without perfume. Drink more water. Tweeze my eyebrows. I am considering adding to this list: shop more often at *p.45*. Everything I've ever bought here instantly makes me feel pretty, and whenever I find myself in this store, Judy and Tricia inspire me to wear more dresses and get a dolled up more often. In general, I take whatever advice these smart and stylish ladies are willing to throw my way.

covet:
brochu walker
philip lim 3.1
mason
rebecca taylor
elijah
inhabit
abigail glaum-lathbury
lara miller

patina

cozy antique and home store

5137 north clark street. between clark and winina. red line: berwyn

773.334.0400 www.patinachicago.com

see website for hours

opened in 2007. owner: alan shull

visa. mc

andersonville > 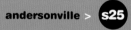 **s25**

Some things get so much better with age (wine and antiques) and some get so much worse (electronics and skin around the neck). Everything in Alan's store, *Patina*, is filled with things that are getting better and cooler with every passing day. Filing cabinets can seem hum drum, but not if they are beautifully patina'd filing cabinets from the University of Wisconsin. Same goes for just about everything in this shop, all which has been carefully chosen by Alan. If only everything aged as well as what can be found here. I'm hoping my neck is listening to me.

covet:
metal cubby
stainless steel kitchen island
university of wisconsin filing cabinet
glass beakers
medicine cabinet
vintage mail sorter
large chalkboard
small maple tree trunk

penelope's

fun clothes for guys and gals

1913 west division street. between wolcott and damen. blue line: division
773.395.2351 www.shoppenelopes.com
mon - sat 11a - 7p sun noon - 6p

opened in 2002. owners: jena frey and joe lauer
all major credit cards accepted
online shopping

wicker park >  **s26**

Recently I was on an overseas flight with a woman wearing a fitted, short dress and stilettos. A few rows back, a girl wore sweats and sneakers. I like to think I fall somewhere in the middle of these two dressing styles (and hopefully not close to either). Finding chic, comfortable travel wear, has always been a challenge—but no longer: *Penelope's* stocks the perfect fun, kicky outfits for travel of any sort—by plane, train, car or foot. Though if you've ever sported stilettos on a transatlantic flight before, this store might not be for you.

covet:
apc
charlotte ronson
plastic island
ella moss
sessun
dolce vita
dunderdon
cheap monday

pivot

eco smart fashion for women

1101 west fulton market. on aberdeen. green / pink lines: clinton
312.243.4754 www.pivotboutique.com
mon 11a - 7p wed - fri 11a - 7p sat 11a - 6p sun noon - 5p

opened in 2007. owner: jessa brinkmeyer
all major credit cards accepted
online shopping

west loop >

Loading up your hybrid with a weeks' worth of recycling to drive to the nearest recycling center because your building doesn't recycle: not fun. Shopping for eco-smart, sustainable and green fashions at *Pivot*: fun! Most of the time doing things for the environment is enjoyable, but Jessa makes it especially so, by making eco fashion actually fashionable. Now that you can look good and save the planet, there are no more excuses—this chic shop ensures that going green never goes out of style.

covet:
noon solar bags
linda loudermilk
stewart + brown
lara miller
toggery
organic john patrick
the midwasteland vintage
frei designs

p.o.s.h.

european flea market style

613 north state street. between ontario and ohio. red line: grand
312.280.1602 www.poshchicago.com
mon - sat 10a - 7p sun 11a - 5p

opened in 1997. owner: karl sorensen
all major credit cards accepted
online shopping

river north >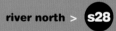

If I were awarding prizes for fan favorite in *eat.shop chicago*, *P.O.S.H.* would win hands down. Anyone I know who has set foot in this store has become instantly infatuated with it. Karl manages to keep things always changing, and has a knack for displaying his European flea market finds in a way that makes you feel like you are right there in Paris or Picadilly bargaining for these desirable items yourself. And what's even better is you don't have to figure out how you're going to carry home a dozen vintage glasses in your carry-on.

covet:
hotel silver
vintage mahjong tiles
etched filigree french glasses
vintage french bingo numbers
ceramic bistro match strike
paint by number kit
french notebooks
cast iron piggy bank

post 27

an urban destination for mid century modern furniture and home goods

1819 west grand avenue. between damen and wood. pink / green lines: ashland-lake
312.829.6122 www.post27store.com
see website for hours

opened in 2008. owners: angela finney-hoffman and barkley hoffman
all major credit cards accepted

west town >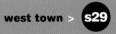

In my travels, I often find myself in stores where three quarters of the store is well put together and merchandised, and a quarter of the store—usually in the back—is a dark and neglected, dusty little area that holds unwanted things. This is not the story at *Post 27*. Every square inch of this store is beautiful and charming, each vintage and modern product draws you in with personal vignettes and stories and little scenes. Store owners, take a lesson from *Post 27*, go forth and revive that ignored back corner of your store that is getting the sorry shaft.

covet:
unison porter sheets
bladon connor's furniture
vintage globes
kindling faceted rocks
vintage trays & glassware
roscoe jackson sawyer bowls
green sawn bench
gail garcia handpainted bowl

quake collectibles

action figure toys and more

4628 north lincoln avenue. between wilson and eastwood. brown line: western
773.878.4288 www.quakecollectibles.net
mon 1 - 6p wed - fri 1 - 6p sat noon - 6 sun noon - 5

opened in 1991. owner: david gutterman
all major credit cards accepted

lincoln square > **s30**

I have a crush on Superheros. It doesn't really matter which one it is (though I prefer Batman and Superman), any supernatural powers and world-saving abilities will do. What's cooler than a super force of good in the face of evil? Some girls wanted a knight in white shining armor, I wanted a man in black tights, a cape and a restrictive head piece. So *Quake Collectibles* is my type of spot, not only for superhero figurines, but action figures of all types—even sports stars. Add in comics, old lunch boxes and Pez and this is a collectors heaven. As for me, I can't stop ogling Spidey.

covet:
comic books
vintage lunch tins
x-men
star wars
spiderman
captain planet
supergirl
pez

171

robin richman

a one-of-a-kind experience

2108 north damen avenue. between charleston and dickens. blue line: damen
773.278.6150 www.robinrichman.com
tue - sat 11a - 6p sun noon - 5p

opened in 1997. owner: robin richman
all major credit cards accepted

bucktown > **s31**

I get many requests from store owners across the country, wanting their business to be considered for the next *eat.shop* book in their city, and they often ask me what I look for in a store. Here it is: I look for the unusual, the unexpected, a passionate owner, and I need to experience a visceral reaction to the place, i.e. it makes me tingle. What does a place like this look like? *Robin Richman*. This is the one and only store of its kind, a mecca for women who want to dress uniquely. Robin and her store are a grand inspiration for anyone wondering what it means to be an outstanding local business.

covet:
gary graham
graham & spencer
johnny farah belts & bags
complex geometries
antipast socks
majestic
marsell
goti

roslyn

classic meets romantic meets modern style

2035 north damen avenue. between dickens and mclean. blue line: damen
773.489.1311 www.roslynboutique.com
tue - sat 11a - 7p sun noon - 5p

opened in 2006. owner: roslyn dulyapaibul
all major credit cards accepted

bucktown > **s32**

I am in the middle of a style crisis. Somewhere in the last year and a half, I lost my style. I'm pretty upset about it, so if you find it, can you let me know? In the meantime, while I'm searching, I'm thinking of starting over at *Roslyn*. Though this store is all about Rosie's style—I'm pretty keen on it, and I thinking of stealing it or rather, swiping my card and paying for it. Rosie's style manages to hit pitch perfect between classic and edgy, dressed-up and dressed-down, romantic and modern—this is just the place to find yourself and your style if it's gone missing, like mine.

covet:
steven alan
trovata
elise bergman
vera wang lavender label
nicholas k
loeffler randall
clu
mackage

scout

scouted vintage pieces

5221 north clark street. between farragut and foster. red line: berwyn
773.275.5700 www.scoutchicago.com
tue - wed 11a - 6p thu - fri noon - 7p sat 11a - 6p sun noon - 5p

opened in 2004. owner: larry vodak
all major credit cards accepted

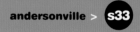

Only a handful of shops have been carried over from the first edition of *eat.shop chicago* to the second, and now on to the third edition. *Scout* is one of them, because whenever I enter Larry's store, I am happily amazed at how his energy and artfulness is never-ending, how he has the ability to sniff out incredible pieces that almost always sell within days of being on the floor, and to present his finds in the most interesting of ways. It's obvious to all that Larry loves what he does, and we the fans love him and *Scout* for all that they bring to Chicago.

covet:
aluminum drinking cans
metal crates
wooden crates
mirrors
red cabinet
black lacquered dresser
ben brandt etchings
reworked vintage lamps

soutache

2125 north damen avenue. between shakespeare and charleston. blue line: damen
773.292.9110 www.soutacheribbons.com
mon by appointment tue - sat 10a - 6p sun noon - 5p

opened in 2005. owner: maili powell
visa. mc
classes. custom orders / design

bucktown > **s34**

I recently bought a sewing machine, and now I'm hyper with a million ideas and projects I'd like to embark on. Who is to blame for this excitement? Maili at *Soutache*, for her store is full of things I must have. I'm so amped, I'm about to start adding ribbons to my running shoes and embellishing my toolbox. And if you feel like you're clumsy with sewing or crafts, yet long for a feathered headband or ribbon-flower brooch, you can either buy one of Maili's own creations, or take a class from the pro herself. Just don't blame me when you become addicted to this store.

covet:
ribbons!
feathers
buttons & more buttons
belt buckles
bag handles
embroidering ribbons
embellishments

sprout home

a garden and home shop

745 north damen avenue. between chicago and superior. cta bus: 66-chicago
312.226.5950 www.sprouthome.com
see website for hours

opened in 2003. owner: tara heibel
all major credit cards accepted
indoor plant design services

ukranian village > s35

I've recently been spending a lot of time in Portland, Oregon, where my parents live. They're both gardeners, so I am completely spoiled by their lush, green garden. When I return to my concrete and glass home in Chicago, I'm reminded that I need some green, and therefore I need *Sprout Home*. It helps my cravings to simply wander through the plants here, and I'm pretty sure that a terrarium filled with succulents will fit right in at my mod condo, yet will still survive the dry, harsh winter. Thank goodness for the green thumbs at *Sprout Home*.

covet:
binth pillows
sunprint kits
tillandsias
stylish bird house
recycled metal wire bird cage
copenhagen terrarium
recycled glass bubble terrarium
bloom in bag

the cottage

homey treasures

5644 north clark street. between olive and hollywood. red line: bryn mawr
773.944.5100
tue - fri noon - 5p sat - sun 11a - 6p

opened in 2009. owner: julie fernstrom
visa. mc

andersonville > 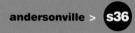s36

I've spent every summer of my life in Northern Michigan, in an old, cozy family cottage. Every summer there is a local "garage sale" called Trash and Treasures. This is an opportunity for everyone to clear out the junk (or unknown gems) that has been hiding in their cottages for years and haul it to the sale. If attending this particular event is outside of your travel perimeter, then *The Cottage* is the next best thing. And where there's never a guarantee of finding something truly great at the sale, *The Cottage* is full of treasures, no trash in sight.

covet:
vintage floral dishes
kitchen towels
baking molds
metal flour & sugar tins
kerr mason jars
vintage floral teacups
garden planters
printed aprons

the sweden shop

designs from scandinavia

3304 west foster avenue. between spaulding and christiana. brown line: kimball
773.478.0327 www.theswedenshop.com
mon - sat 10a - 6p sun 10a - 3p

opened in 1950. owner: patti rasmussen
visa. mc

albany park > s37

I have had such an itch to go to Scandinavia. Copenhagen, Stockholm and Oslo are all at the top of my travel list, and my main motivation is the design sensibilities of this part of the globe. Until I can satisfy my yen by hopping on a flight, I can just hop up north to *The Sweden Shop*. Talk about going to the source. This place carries a collection of all of the rock stars of Scandinavian art and design, from Carl Laarsen to Lotta Jansdotter, so you get a taste of both the old and new schools of design. Visiting here is a perfect primer to get me ready for my hopefully-in-the-near-future trip.

covet:
lotta jansdotter
royal copenhagen
bodum
anne black
tord boontje
marimekko
orrefors
kosta boda

tula

effortlessly sophisticated women's clothing

3738 north southport avenue. between grace and waveland. brown line: southport
773.549.2876 www.tulaboutique.com
mon - wed 11a - 6p thu - fri 11a - 7p sat 11a - 6p sun noon - 5p

opened in 2006. owners: sue and laura westgate
all major credit cards accepted
online shopping

lakeview > **s38**

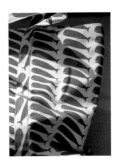

When I was shooting *Tula*, Laura was designing her window display with a theme that honored the upcoming summer reading season. She stacked piles of beloved books, hung book pages that she had stitched together, and dressed a mannequin in the perfect seasonal outfit for reading in a hammock. Though it was barely summer, Laura's creative window had me hankering for summer days and the clothing I could wear during them. I could have bought everything in the store at that moment.

covet:
nicole fahri everything
allude italian knitwear
majestic t's
bo'em plage sandals
virginia johnson scarves & bags
inhabit sweaters
organic by john patrick
hache

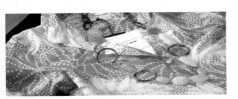

urban remains

antique architectural artifacts

410 north paulina street. between hubbard and kinzie. pink / green lines: ashland-lake
312.492.6254 www.urbanremainschicago.com
mon - sat 11a - 6p sun noon - 5p

opened in 2006. owner: eric j. nordstrom
all major credit cards accepted
online shopping

west loop >

Do you sometimes wonder what will remain of this city in a hundred years? Will it be like "Wall-E," where our garbage will have overtaken everything and we'll have to leave earth to live on a spaceship? I hope not. I'm hoping that instead, there will be amazing places like *Urban Remains*, that people can buy and repurpose the greatest hits of architecture, technology, furniture, signage, lighting and miscellany. Recycling and re-using via a cool shop like *Urban Remains* seems a much better way to manage our throw-aways than letting it all pile up, doesn't it?

covet:
'20s light fixtures
exterior building elements
antique mantles
vintage signs
millwork
period hardware
leaded glass windows
salvaged doors

zap props & antiques

fabulous miscellany for rent
3611 south loomis place. off of 37th. bus #35: iron street
773.376.2278 www.zapprops.com
mon - thu 9a - 5p fri 8a - 3p

opened in 1989. owner: bill rawski
all major credit cards accepted
rentals. design services

south chicago > s40

Please don't get too attached to any of the items you see in these photos: it's more than likely that you can't buy them. You can, however, rent them. I know, I know, I'm pushing it—this isn't *eat.shop.rent chicago*—but I was so wowed by this place, I wanted to spread the word. Though *Zap Props* does have a selection of for-sale items, the bulk of the stuff here is for borrowing only. While I don't know why you might want to rent a clown, an old telephone, or a Coca-Cola sign, I'm pretty sure you creative types out there will think of something.

covet:
for rent:
  telephones
  typewriters
  factory signs
  diner decor
  general store items
  mid-century mod tvs
frames & framing services

etc.

the eat.shop guides were created by kaie wellman and are published by cabazon books

eat.shop chicago 3rd edition was written, researched and photographed by anna h. blessing

editing: kaie wellman   copy editing: susanne frank   fact checking: michaela cotter santen
map and layout production: meagan gall

anna thx: all of the businesses in this book, kaie, shawn and everyone who helped along the way

photo of frank sinatra is a close up shot of his "come dance with me!" album cover

cabazon books: eat.shop chicago 3rd edition
ISBN-13 9780982325438

every effort has been made to ensure the accuracy of the information in this book. however, certain details are subject to change. please remember when using the guides that hours alter seasonally and sometimes sadly, businesses close. the publisher cannot accept responsibility for any consequences arising from the use of this book.

the eat.shop guides are distributed by independent publishers group: www.ipgbook.com

to peer further into the world of eat.shop and to buy books, please visit: www.eatshopguides.com

PRINTED IN SOUTH KOREA